Easy Crafts for Kids

CRAFT WITH RECYCLING

A KID'S GUIDE TO CREATING WITH UPCYCLED MATERIALS

Lucimari
Translated by
Grace McQuillan

SKY PONY PRESS · NEW YORK

CONTENTS

HANDY HOLDERS

JUG MASK

HOORAY FOR SPRING!

WOODEN FIGURINES

WOVEN NOTEBOOK

GENTLE JELLYFISH

FUNNY FACES

CAPTURED CREATURE

A Word from the Artist

I'm a graphic designer and artist and I've loved crafting ever since I was a child. I like nothing better than giving my imagination free rein and cutting out, gluing, and tinkering with all kinds of things! To me, a sheet of beautiful drawing paper is just as much fun to work with as a page torn out of a magazine, and the same is true no matter what kind of material I'm using. Whether they're high-quality or not, I enjoy mixing and matching whatever objects I have on hand to create something new. I don't plan anything ahead of time. Instead, I find inspiration in the infinite palette of colors, textures, and shapes in the materials I've collected and this is what spurs my imagination to design something dreamlike and elegant.

Recycling is a tremendously important part of my work as an artist because, for me, it's a true source of creativity. Today, I lead eco-friendly art workshops for children as a way to share my passion for this kind of artistic creation with them.

"Nothing goes to waste—everything is transformed." Now it's your turn to give your trash a new life!

Lucimari

TIPS AND TRICKS

EIGHT PROJECTS: EIGHT UNIQUE WORKS OF ART!

You already know how important recycling is. These projects offer you a fun alternative to recycling in the usual way: instead of just sorting and getting rid of your paper and plastic, you can give these things a second life by transforming them into works of art!

In this book, we're going to be using materials like paper, cardboard, fabric scraps, leftover balls of yarn, and spare beads and buttons. These projects will teach you how to use all kinds of objects in ways you may have never seen before!

Whenever we're creating art out of recycled materials, one person's end result can look very different from someone else's. Don't worry if you need to adapt the ideas in this book to what you're able to find and what you want to make. Imagination has a very important place in these creations. You're the artist!

BEFORE YOU GET STARTED, HERE'S A LITTLE ADVICE . . .

● If you want to be ready for these activities, you're going to have to start **collecting**! Little by little, start setting aside bulkier items that you want to recycle in a large box and use a shoebox to save smaller objects like magazines, boxes of all kinds (egg cartons, round wooden cheese boxes, cookie or cereal boxes, etc.), plastic caps, plastic bottles, yogurt containers, balls of yarn, fabric, beads, buttons, ribbon, etc.

● As far as **paper** goes, my advice is to hold onto all of your drawings—especially the ones you think aren't good enough to keep. Just paint over them with a roller and use them for something else! You can also recycle unused paper from your school notebooks by gently taking them apart and separating the pages.

● You can buy **glue** at an arts and crafts store and you'll probably find plenty of use for it even after you finish these eight projects. Both white and clear glue can be applied with a paintbrush and will dry quickly, but you can't use them on plastic. If you can get one, a glue gun is easy to use and can be used on all surfaces. The glue dries quickly and won't drip. If you do use a glue gun, just make sure not to put your fingers on the hot tip!

● Remember to **wash your hands** regularly. This will keep your materials clean and make it easier for you to pick up and manipulate the various parts of your creations.

TOOLS

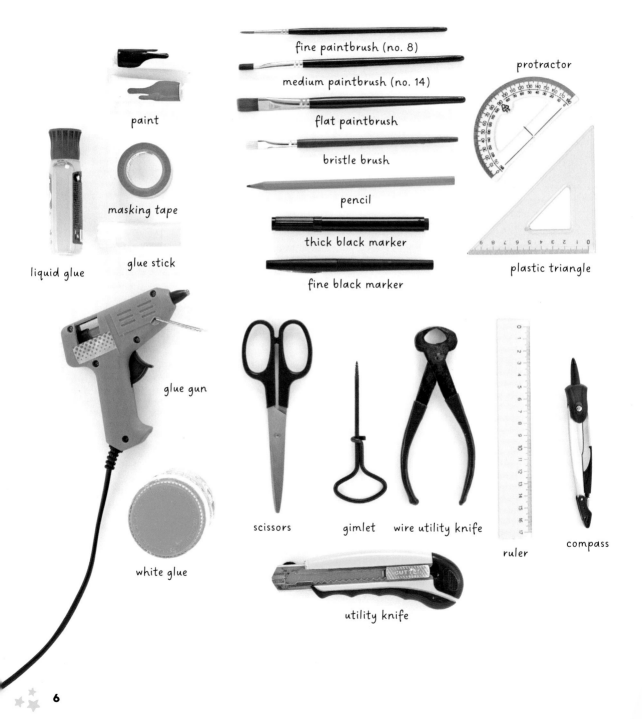

fine paintbrush (no. 8)

medium paintbrush (no. 14)

flat paintbrush

bristle brush

pencil

thick black marker

fine black marker

protractor

plastic triangle

paint

masking tape

liquid glue

glue stick

glue gun

white glue

scissors

gimlet

wire utility knife

ruler

compass

utility knife

MATERIALS

round wooden cheese box lid

cork

toothpicks

string

ribbon

beads

plastic caps   buttons

fabric scraps

wood pieces

yarn

plastic bottles

jars with lids

tin cans

laundry detergent bottles

egg cartons

old plastic folders or sheet protectors, thick brown cardboard, thin cardboard (cereal boxes, cookie boxes)

white paper, graph paper, and colored paper

magazine pages, wrapping paper

HANDY HOLDERS

HANDY HOLDERS

If you're someone who likes creating things, you may often find yourself with far too many pencils, markers, and paintbrushes. These items need to be organized and separated so they stay in good condition and are easy to find. Have you had enough of your parents asking you to tidy up? Then this project will help you out!

TOOLS

1 pencil

Liquid glue

1 glue gun (or strong glue)

1 flat paintbrush

1 ruler

1 plastic triangle

MATERIALS

- 1 piece of thick cardboard
- Paint (acrylic or gouache)
- 3 small tin cans (here we're using 14-ounce (400 g) cans)
- Leftover yarn scraps

1

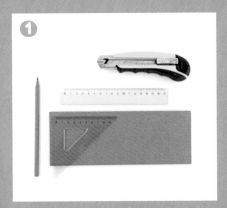

On your piece of cardboard, draw and cut out a 9 1/2 x 3 1/2 inch (24 x 9 cm) rectangle. You can adjust these measurements based on how much space your cans need when they are lined up next to each other.

2

Paint one side of your cardboard base any color you like.

3

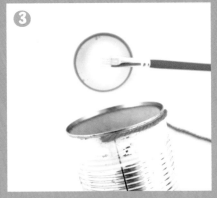

Apply white glue around the top of one can. Gently press one end of your piece of yarn onto the glue.

4

Wrap the yarn around the can wherever you have applied glue. Make sure there are no gaps between the rows of yarn. Add more glue as you go.

5

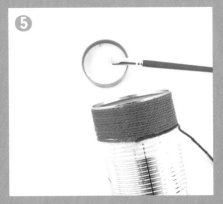

When you want to change colors, just cut the yarn. Then apply more glue and attach the end of your second piece of yarn.

6

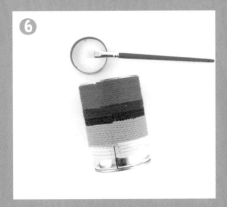

You can switch colors as many times as you want, but make sure you always attach the end of your new piece of yarn to the same side of the can as the others.

Repeat these steps for the two other cans.

Apply glue to the bottom of each can and attach the cans to your base. Press down firmly.

OTHER IDEAS

- For a special occasion, why not give a friend or family member a flowerpot? You can easily decorate the cans using cloth or woven paper, too (see "Woven Notebook" on p. 37).
- You could also make a bank out of a coffee can—just cut a slit in the lid. To decorate it, try colorful tape, ribbon, or pieces of old plastic folders/sheet protectors.

TIP

● To prevent gaps between your lines of yarn, try not to pull on the yarn when you're wrapping it around the can. Just lay it on top of the glue and follow the rows that are already in place.

JUG MASK

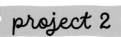

project 2

JUG MASK

Behind every bottle of laundry detergent . . . is a glorious mask!
What will yours look like? A funny character, a robot, an animal?
Let your imagination run wild!

TOOLS

1 pair of
scissors

1 utility knife

1 glue gun
(or strong glue)

MATERIALS

- 1 laundry detergent bottle
- Plastic bottle caps, corks, beads, buttons, nuts and bolts, yogurt containers, etc.
- 1 strip of cardboard
- Scraps of ribbon, yarn, string, mesh produce bags, fabric, etc.

1

Look at your bottle and think about how you want to transform it. Make a simple sketch and then adjust things if you need to once you start assembling your mask.

2

Use scissors or a utility knife* to cut the front and back faces of the bottle to form two beautiful ears.

3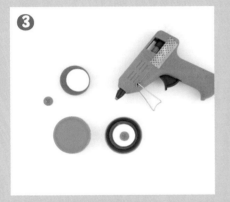

Next, make your creature's eyes out of whatever materials you'd like. Here, for instance, I've glued buttons onto bottle caps.

4

Now make the mouth using a large piece of plastic like a yogurt container or lid.

5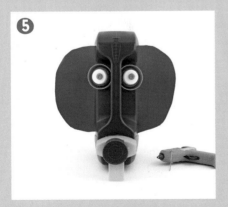

Glue the eyes and mouth onto the bottle.

6

Add smaller objects to your character's face to give it more personality. Start by decorating the ears.

17

* Ask an adult to help you with this part.

Now decorate the cheeks to make the face really pop.

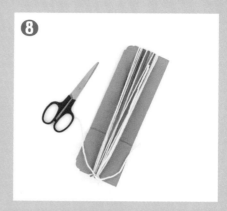

To make the hair, first find or cut a strip of cardboard that matches how long you want the hair to be. Then wrap the yarn around the piece of cardboard. Use a separate piece of yarn to tie a knot around the yarn at one end of the cardboard strip. At the other end of the cardboard strip, cut the yarn.

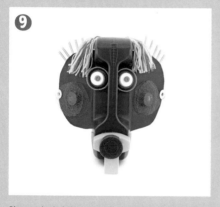

Glue on the hair. You can adjust the length by trimming the yarn like a hairdresser.

Now you can finish off your mask with a stylish hat!

> ≥ **TIP** ≤
> ● Try to collect anything you might need for the jug mask before you start the project. You'll have more objects to choose from, and that's what will stimulate your imagination! Decorate a large shoe box and store your materials inside.

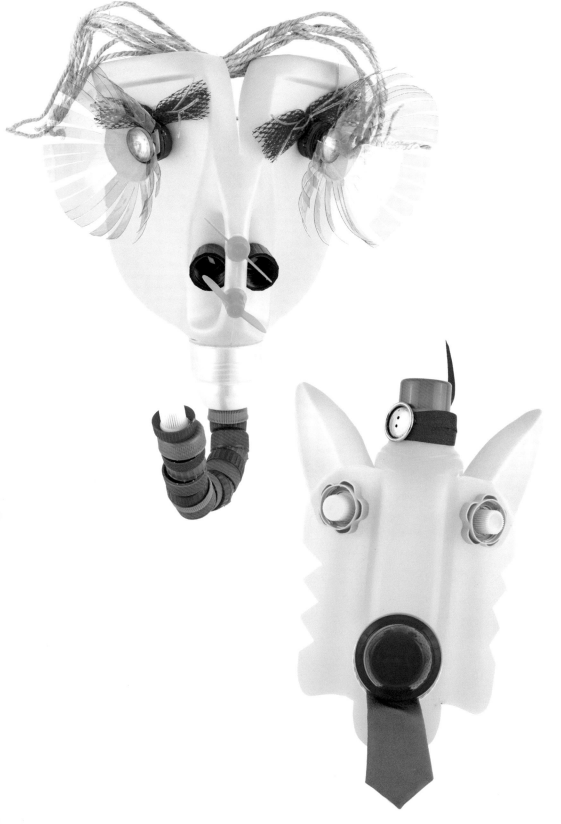

HOORAY FOR SPRING!

Jump into spring and create your own beautiful branch adorned with colorful flowers. Whether you're celebrating the arrival of the first buds or trying to hang on until the last gray winter days are over, this project is sure to brighten up your living room walls!

TOOLS

1 bristle brush

1 pair of scissors

1 utility knife

White glue

MATERIALS

- 4 half-dozen egg cartons in various colors
- 1 piece of brown cardboard
- **Paint** (acrylic or gouache)

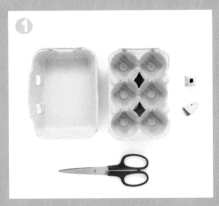

Cut the egg cartons in half so you have four lids and four bottoms. Then cut off the two points in the center of each carton.

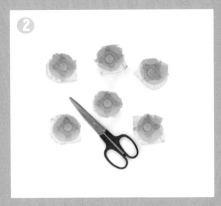

Cut out each small egg "container" (the hollow parts). Repeat with the three other cartons.

Make four cuts in each small egg container to create your flower petals.

Gently separate the petals from each other and trim them to look like your favorite flowers.

Draw several leaves of different shapes and sizes on the flat part of the lid, then cut them out.

Now it's time to create pistils for your flowers using the cardboard points you removed earlier. Feel free to cut some of them into different shapes to make each flower blossom unique!

If you want to, you can paint the petals, leaves, and pistils a brighter color. Depending on the color of your egg cartons, you may not need to paint everything.

Now stack your petals together to make the blossoms for your branch. Glue the layers on top of each other then add the pistils.

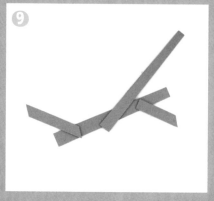

Use a utility knife* to cut strips of brown cardboard that are 0.75 inch (2 cm) wide and several different lengths. Choose one long branch and glue the smaller branches to it.

Arrange your leaves and flowers on the branch to find the composition that looks best. When you like the design, glue everything onto the branch.

> ≥ **TIP** ≤
> ● You don't necessarily need to paint all of your leaf and flower pieces. Egg cartons sometimes come in blue, purple, green, and even yellow—see what you can find and play around with the colors!

* Always be extremely careful when using a utility knife.

⧼ OTHER IDEAS ⧽

- Instead of using the cardboard points to make the pistils, feel free to swap them out for buttons, scraps of yarn, bottle caps, or even large beads.

WOODEN FIGURINES

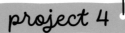
project 4

WOODEN FIGURINES

You used to love playing with your wooden building blocks, but then you grew up. . . .
Now's the time to give them a second life! Use all of those amazing shapes to build
yourself a posse of colorful, silly-faced figurines.

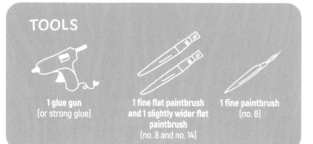

TOOLS

1 glue gun
(or strong glue)

1 fine flat paintbrush
and 1 slightly wider flat
paintbrush
(no. 8 and no. 14)

1 fine paintbrush
(no. 8)

MATERIALS

- Wooden building blocks, painted or natural wood color
- Several paint colors
- Masking tape

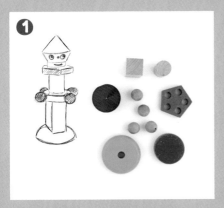

Take a careful look at your wooden blocks. Try imagining what your future figurines might look like, then make a few basic sketches.

Using a flat paintbrush, paint the whole surface of your blocks with whatever colors you like.

For a bright, vibrant color, go ahead and apply two or three layers of paint. Let your pieces dry completely.

Use a flat paintbrush and masking tape to add colorful horizontal or vertical bands (see tip, p. 34).

If you have any round blocks, you can paint the top and bottom faces a different color.

Build your figurine, but don't glue the pieces together yet. Before you do any decorating, take a good look at it.

Use the technique explained in the tip box below if you want to paint triangles on your blocks.

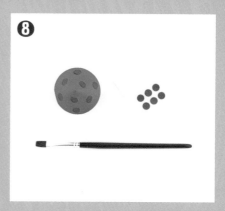

For evenly spaced dots, press round stickers onto the block before painting it. Remove the stickers when the paint is dry.

If you want to give your figurine a facial expression, add eyes and a mouth using a fine paintbrush.

Use the glue gun to build your figurine from the bottom up. Leave any small hanging decorations (like the balls in the picture) for the end.

TIP

• If you want to add horizontal or vertical bands—or geometric shapes like triangles—using masking tape will give you the best results. You'll be able to see exactly where you need to paint. Remove the tape when the paint is dry.

WOVEN NOTEBOOK

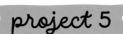

WOVEN NOTEBOOK

Do you like drawing, writing stories, or keeping a journal?
Are you all of a sudden out of notebooks? Well, don't worry, you can
make one! Once the pages are put together, you can design a unique cover
that's just right for whatever you're thinking of putting inside it.

TOOLS

1 pencil

1 glue stick

White glue

1 plastic triangle

1 ruler

1 bristle brush

1 pair of scissors

1 utility knife

MATERIALS

- **6 sheets of A4** (8.5 x 11) **paper** (make sure you have a few different colors and styles: white, colored, painted, grid paper, etc.)

- **Other kinds of paper for the weaving** (magazine pages, newspaper, wrapping paper)

- **2 pieces of cardboard** (the two biggest sides of a cereal box would be perfect)

- **2 pieces of ribbon, 8 inches** (20 cm) **long**

- **1 piece of yarn or cotton string, 20 inches** (50 cm) **long**

① Cut the magazine pages into 18 strips that are 0.4 to 0.8 inches (1–2 cm) wide.

② Lay one strip on the table horizontally. Glue another strip on top of it to form a right angle, then glue a second vertical strip underneath it.

③ Glue on half of the remaining strips vertically, alternating over and under the horizontal strip. Leave 1 millimeter between each strip.

④ Now continue by weaving horizontal strips under and over the vertical strips.

⑤ Fold the six sheets of paper into fourths. Stack the sheets inside of each other so they look like the pages of a book. Use a utility knife* to trim the three outer edges (0.1-inch (3-mm) maximum). Now you have your notebook. Measure it.

* Be very careful when using the utility knife.

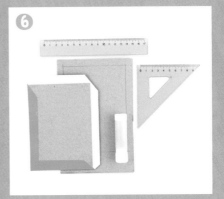

⑥ Cut one piece of cardboard into two rectangles the same size as your notebook. Glue them onto whatever kind of paper you like (newspaper, magazine, wrapping paper) leaving a 0.4-inch (1 cm) border around the edge. Cut the corners then fold down and glue the excess paper to the cardboard.

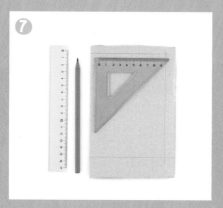

Fold the other piece of cardboard in half. Use the plastic triangle to make a mark perpendicular to that fold. Now add 0.2 inches (5 mm) to the measurements of your notebook pages and draw a rectangle that size. Cut out this rectangle.

Turn over your weaving. Use white glue to attach the cardboard rectangle you just cut out.

Trim the ends of your woven strips so they are all the same length. Glue down any stray ends around the edges.

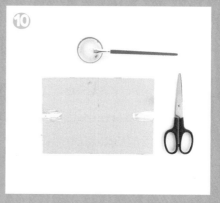

Now turn over the cover. Glue on two ribbons: one in the center of each outer edge.

Pick up the two pieces of cardboard that you covered with paper in step 6. Glue them to the inside of your notebook cover on top of the ribbons. Press down and let dry underneath a stack of books.

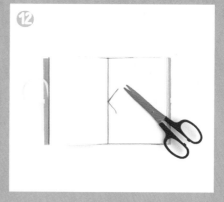

Place your notebook pages inside the cover and tie everything together with cotton string. Tie a double knot and cut off any excess string.

TIPS

- You can dress up your covers with fabric, wrapping paper, a collage, or even your own drawings.
- If you don't want to attach ribbons to your notebook, you can keep it closed with a rubber band.

GENTLE JELLYFISH

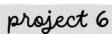

project 6

GENTLE JELLYFISH

If you're as fascinated by the graceful jellyfish as I am,
then I think you'll love transforming your plastic bottles into these
delicate, translucent sea creatures and hanging them up at home.
And hopefully, one day, plastic bottles won't be thrown
into the ocean anymore!

TOOLS

1 gimlet

1 pair of
scissors

1 utility knife

MATERIALS

- 2 plastic bottles with their caps (bottles should be two different colors, if possible)
- 2 old plastic folders/sheet protectors
- 1 piece of nylon string (or white/colored string), 20 inches (50 cm) long
- 1 medium bead
- 1 roll of clear tape or masking tape

1. Cut both bottles into three pieces (bottom, middle, and top) using a utility knife.* Keep the two top parts and one bottle bottom.

2. Cut 0.4-inch (1 cm) strips into both top parts. Stop each cut around 1.25 to 2 inches (3 to 5 cm) below the bottle cap.

3. Fold down the strips, opening them like the petals of a flower. Press down firmly at the place where you stopped cutting.

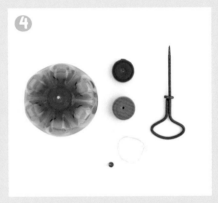

4. Use the gimlet* to pierce a hole in both caps and in the center of the bottle bottom (ask an adult to help you). Attach the bead to one end of the nylon string.

5. Cut the sheet protectors/plastic folders into 18 strips that are 0.4 inches (1 cm) wide. Use whatever colors you want!

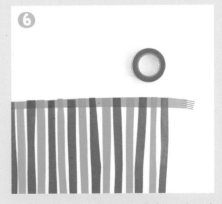

6. Lay one strip on the table horizontally. Secure the ends with tape. Now place the other strips on top of it vertically, leaving 1 to 2 millimeters between each one.

* Be very careful when using the utility knife and the gimlet.

Attach the vertical strips to the horizontal strip with tape. Remove the whole thing from the table and cut off any extra tape.

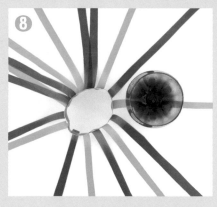

Make a ring of tentacles that is slightly wider than the diameter of the bottle bottom.

Insert the ring into the bottle bottom, then tape it to the inside of the bottle.

Thread the string through the neck of one bottle, then through the hole in the matching bottle cap. Screw the cap onto the bottle.

Repeat this process with the other bottle and its cap. Try not to let the string slip while you're doing this!

Now pass the string through the hole in the bottle bottom (the piece with tentacles). Pull the thread to make sure it is taut and use tape to attach it to the outside of the bottle bottom.

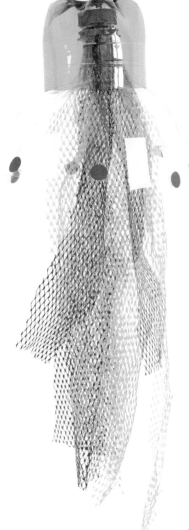

TIP

- You can replace the sheet protectors/plastic folders with mesh produce bags cut into wide strips. Just tie your strips together with a long piece of string and they're ready to use!

FUNNY FACES

Here's a two-part project that brings together creativity and play.
These African-inspired cardboard masks can be very expressive and are
perfect for having fun with friends and family. Now you just have to
decide if you'll give them a silly face . . . or a scary one!

TOOLS

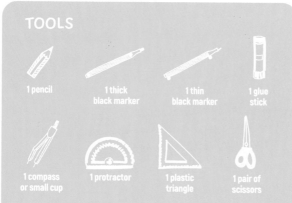

1 pencil

1 thick
black marker

1 thin
black marker

1 glue
stick

1 compass
or small cup

1 protractor

1 plastic
triangle

1 pair of
scissors

MATERIALS

- 3 sheets of white paper
- 2 sheets of colored paper (recycled or painted)
- 4 pieces of thin cardboard (like pizza boxes) (no more than 2 mm thick)
- 3 bases for your masks (cardboard, wood, Styrofoam, Plexiglass, etc.) around 12 x 12 inches (30 x 30 cm) in size

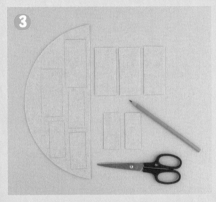

Use a compass and/or plastic triangle to draw seven geometric shapes in pencil on a thin piece of cardboard. Follow the picture above and make sure you have two different sizes for a few of your shapes. Be sure to include a small and large rectangle. Your shapes should be 1.5 to 2.5 inches (4 to 6 cm) long and 1.25 to 2.5 inches (3 to 6 cm) tall.

Roughly cut around your shapes, then carefully cut along the lines you traced. You now have seven templates.

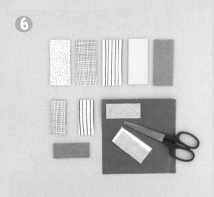

Use your templates to trace five small and five large rectangles. Do the same with your other templates until you have ten of each shape.

Cut out and group the shapes.

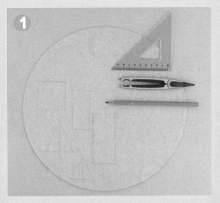

Take two pieces of white paper and use a black marker to draw different graphic motifs, like dots, stripes, or lines on each one.

Glue a few rectangles to the back of one of the sheets of paper you just decorated. Cut off any extra paper around the edges. Do the same with your colored paper and all but two of the other rectangles. Don't glue anything to the last two rectangles.

7

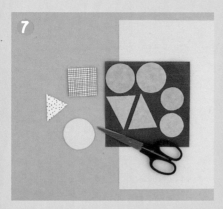

Repeat this process with your other shapes. Remember to leave two of each shape bare.

8

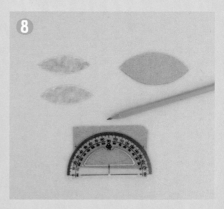

For the eyes and mouth, you will need two sets of ovals. One set should be 3 inches (8 cm) long and the other two should be 2.5 inches (6 cm) long. Use a protractor to draw the rounded edges.

9

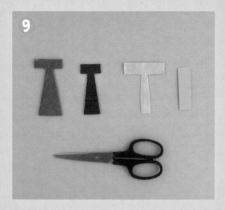

Draw and cut out four different noses. Repeat step 6 with colored paper but leave two noses bare.

10

For the eyes, cut out four small circles using scraps of white paper. Each one should be about 0.6 inches (1.5 cm) in diameter. Add pupils with a black marker.

11

Next, cut out the base for your mask (cardboard, Styrofoam, etc.). Need ideas? Here are a few that work well: a 10-inch (25 cm) circle, a 12 x 7-inch (30 x 18 cm) rectangle, or an oval.

12

And the rest is up to you! The rules are simple: just choose a base and make a face!

⇒ TIPS ⇐

- This is a project that requires a lot of cutting, so don't hesitate to ask your family or friends for help!
- Take photos of the different faces you make, then print them out to make a fun little gallery. You could even invite people you know to an art exhibit in your own home!

CAPTURED
CREATURE

CAPTURED CREATURE

Did you know that all four of a butterfly's wings are covered in microscopic scales? We may not be able to see these scales with the naked eye, but we can certainly admire these insects' sumptuous wings. In this activity, your job is to capture the most beautiful butterfly of all!

TOOLS

- 1 pencil
- Liquid glue
- 1 glue gun
- Wire cutters
- 1 plastic triangle
- 1 bristle brush
- 1 stapler
- 1 flat paintbrush no. 14
- 1 ruler
- 1 pair of scissors

MATERIALS

- Paint
- 1 cardboard cereal box (the two larger sides)
- 1 egg carton
- 1 cork
- 1 large jar with lid
- 1 round wooden cheese box lid (look for something between 4 and 4.5 inches in diameter, like camembert boxes)
- 1 toothpick
- Fabric scraps
- Beads and buttons (no wider than 0.4 inches (1 cm))
- Yarn

1

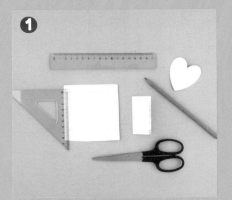

On a piece of cardboard, use the plastic triangle to draw two 2.5 x 2.5-inch (6.5 cm by 6.5 cm) squares. Cut them out and fold them in half. Draw half of a heart shape on each one, then cut along the lines. You should now have two hearts.

2

Glue your hearts onto the fabric scraps. Cut off any fabric that extends beyond the cardboard. Repeat this step on the other side of both hearts.

3

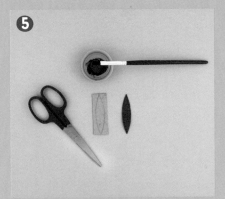

Use your jar to trace a circle on the flat part of the egg carton lid. Cut out the circle. This will be your base.

4

Take your cork and slice off a 0.4-inch (1 cm) piece. Glue the slice of cork onto your base, paint both of them, then place this base inside the jar lid.

5

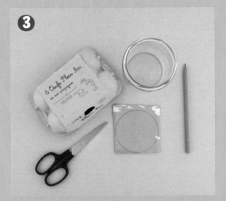

Now draw and cut out the body of your butterfly: a thin oval 2.75 inches (7 cm) long and around 0.4 inches (1 cm) wide. Use any color you like to paint the body on both sides.

6

Glue one set of wings on top of the other, making sure both sets are still bent slightly in half. The points of the hearts should be facing in opposite directions.

7

Decorate your butterfly with buttons and beads, making sure the wings are symmetrical. You can add a strip of yarn to give the butterfly body a velvety look.

8

Now attach the body to the wings using your glue gun. Keep the wings straight on top of the body while the glue dries so they don't end up leaning too much to one side.

9

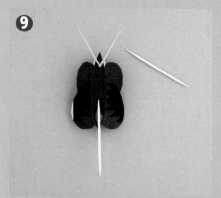

Cut two antennae from your egg carton and glue them to your butterfly. Then glue a toothpick to the underside of your butterfly's body and press it into the cork.

10

Use wire cutters* to cut and remove the staples from the round cheese box lid. You should now have a circular wooden band.

11

Trim this wooden band until it fits around the mouth of your jar. Gently slide your butterfly into the jar and screw on the lid.

12

Staple the resized wooden band and use it to hide the jar lid.

* Be very careful when using the wire cutters.